THINGS TO DO NOW THAT YOU'RE SINGLE *AGAIN*

things to do now

EVA GIZOWSKA   Illustrations by Robyn Neild

that you're
single *again*

MQP

contents

seize
the moment

Breaking up is hard. No matter who instigated the split, suddenly a huge part of your life has changed for ever. All sorts of emotions may come to the surface – sadness, anger, regret, guilt, confusion, fear, loneliness. You're on your own now – and that can feel scary. But you've got a choice. You don't have to remain stuck in your misery. Of course, feelings don't just go away over night. But if you're brave, you can create a great new future for yourself. The first step is to seize every moment. You might not feel like it right now, but if you look around, you will discover countless opportunities for happiness.

If you want your life to move on, you need to be open-hearted. This means being receptive to new experiences, people and opportunities.

Trust and let go. Before something new can come in, you first need to let go of the old. This applies to new relationships. If you want to make emotional space for someone new, you need to stop dwelling on the past. If you can't do that, it could be that you're not quite ready to move on yet.

Brighten up your weekend and throw a party at short notice. Call your friends and ask everyone to bring a bottle and a surprise guest. The day before, blitz-clean your home and buy drinks and party snacks that are easy to prepare. On the night, make sure you're looking your best. Put on some great music and dim the lights – or light candles – to create a more flattering ambience.

Evening classes can sound a little nerdy. But you really shouldn't knock them until you've tried pottery, silk-screen printing, Italian for beginners, creative writing or black-and-white photography. You might be surprised to discover you have a real talent that's never been tapped into before. It's also a great way to make some new friends.

Don't sit at home watching a DVD on your own. Invite some friends round for an impromptu screening, with popcorn and ice cream.

Next time you go to a party, flirt like mad, and dance like crazy. The great thing about being single is that you don't have to worry about a cranky, jealous partner who's sulking in the corner because you're not paying him/her enough attention.

Get your adrenaline going by trying a white-knuckle experience such as white-water rafting, hang-gliding, hot-air ballooning or rock climbing.

Jump on a last-minute flight or train to a city you've never been to before. There's no partner to hold you back now.

> Accept the risk and then reap the rewards.
> ANON

Enjoy the fact that you're a free spirit and fly a kite on a windy day.

Instead of mulling over the Sunday papers on your own, arrange to meet a friend in a nearby café and enjoy going through them together over a lazy brunch.

Head for the nearest beach and work on that sun-kissed glow.

You don't need a partner to go punting on the river, eat strawberries and cream or drink champagne on a hot summer's day. You can have just as much fun with friends.

Life only ever exists in each moment. If you spend your moments worrying about the past or the future, life will simply pass you by. But if you can learn to enjoy each moment for what it is without looking backwards or forwards all the time, you will experience greater peace of mind and contentment.

Having a good clear-out can be amazingly therapeutic – no matter what else is going on in your life. Getting rid of all the junk in your home is a good way to regain a sense of control.

Every day, plan something pleasurable to do. It could be talking to a friend, reading a good book, listening to music or seeing a good play. By becoming absorbed in enjoyable activities, you're less likely to worry about being single.

Keep in touch. Start a regular monthly get-together with three or four friends. Choose an evening – for example, the first Friday of every month – and take it in turns to meet at each other's homes. Keep it simple. Get a few bottles of wine and order a big pizza to share.

Rent a cottage in the country
for the weekend with some
friends. Take walking boots
so you can go on long,
invigorating hikes.

Spend an evening chatting
with friends in front of an
open fire.

Do you really want to look back on your life and see how wonderful it could have been had you not been afraid to live it?
CAROLINE MYSS

Go mountain- or hill-walking and stop and stare at the stunning views.

Pick up the phone and call a friend you haven't spoken to for months.

Jump on a bus that goes to a local area you've never been to before, and spend a few hours exploring. You never know who your new companions might be.

Get up early and go to a Sunday market. You never know what bargains – or who – you might find.

Now's your chance to be more proactive. Throw a street party and get to know those who live around you better.

Sometimes, if you want to break out of a rut, you've just got to break the rules.

Do something different in your lunch hour. Visit an art gallery or museum, or if there isn't one nearby, go for a walk in a park. You'll return to the office feeling much more refreshed than if you'd just had a sandwich at your desk, or in the local café.

Set off early and walk to work on a bright, sunny day. You never know who you might meet along the way.

Have a picnic. Pack some delicious sandwiches, salad, fruit and a bottle of chilled white wine, invite friends to share your feast and head off to an idyllic spot.

Link up with some old friends you haven't seen for a while and go to an open-air music festival.

Apply to be an extra in a film. If you're lucky, you'll earn some money and have a lot of fun. And you never know who you might meet.

Mark the beginning of a brand new era by planting a tree, a tomato plant or a rose bush and watch it grow.

Be daring. Go to the funfair on your own. There's no one to see you making a fool of yourself. So, try all the rides, eat candyfloss and scream when you're scared!

Take up an activity you've always wanted to try but never got round to when you were with your partner. For example, painting, learning to play an instrument or horse-riding.

Throw a fancy-dress party.

Treat yourself to the latest bestselling novel, then snuggle up in bed and read until 2a.m. if you feel like it.

Use your time alone to do some of the things you used to do before you met your partner. For example, get some sexy cycling shorts and go cycling. If you haven't got a bike any more, borrow or hire one.

Release all those pent-up emotions by putting your feelings down on paper. You'll feel much better afterwards.

Not keen on cooking for one? Now is the perfect time to develop your culinary skills and experiment with new recipes. Use lots of unusual ingredients, herbs and spices, and try out your new repertoire on friends.

If you want to meet someone new, spread the word and let friends know.

Being single means you can be so much more spontaneous. If you want to see a play or a film on the spur of the moment, you can just buy a last-minute ticket without having to check your partner's schedule.

Go rollerblading in the park. It doesn't matter if you can't do it. Half the fun is trying. You never know who you might bump into ... literally.

Relish your chance to let go of responsibility. Go to the zoo and enjoy this time to be totally carefree.

Invite friends over for a game of table tennis.

Join a yoga class and get in the best shape you can be. It will help you relax if you're feeling stressed about splitting up, too.

Join a ballroom dancing class and learn to foxtrot, samba and tango. Focusing on all those new steps is a brilliant way to stop dwelling on the past.

Put on some music while you do your chores. Listening to tunes you like as you do the ironing and cleaning will make it seem much easier and you'll whizz through it in double-quick time.

Find someone to play badminton with and have a few games.

Start a book, film or theatre club (or any club based on a common theme) and meet once a month to discuss a book, or see a film or play, and then talk about it afterwards.

Make a list of quirky things you'd like to do now that you have the time, such as learn to play bridge, throw a boomerang, make the perfect lemon mousse, dive off a diving board, stand under a waterfall, ice-skate backwards ... Try to tick at least one thing off your list every month.

" It's just such a freeing thing to set great
challenges for yourself, to travel, to learn
more about the world, to just go out there
and get crazy and get free and get strong. "
ANGELINA JOLIE

*Spend a warm, sunny afternoon
people-watching at a pavement café.
Wonder at the world as it goes by.*

" *Life is about not knowing, having to change,
taking the moment and making the best of it,
without knowing what's going to happen next.
Delicious ambiguity.* "
GILDA RADNER

Avoid feeling lonely at the weekend by planning activities. Rent a houseboat with friends, or organize a barbecue, a trip to the cinema or a sporting event such as a game of softball, volleyball or football.

Remind yourself what it feels like to be a child. Take a godchild, nephew or niece, or friend's child off his or her parents' hands for the day and go to an adventure playground; follow this with ice-cream cornets.

Get a telescope and search the skies for a comet on a clear night. Then wish upon a star.

Celebrate the seasons with friends. Make a bonfire and toast some marshmallows when the autumn leaves arrive; have an Easter egg hunt to welcome spring.

Make the most of it. There's no one banging on the bathroom door now, so stock up on pampering bath products and take a long, candlelit bath.

Invite friends to go somewhere exotic to celebrate your next birthday. It will make a change from another night at that 'great little bar' – that you've been to a million times – at the end of your road.

Test your mettle and put your practical skills to good use. Get out into the countryside and, instead of booking into a cosy hotel or B&B, pitch a tent and spend the night under the stars. There's no need to go it alone. See if you can talk an adventurous friend into joining you.

Look up some old schoolfriends and take a trip down memory lane. Hire a venue and organize a good old-fashioned school reunion.

Have a ruthless rummage through your belongings.
Make a pile of everything you don't need, then team
up with a friend and take it all to a car-boot sale.
Spend the proceeds on something you truly want.

*People love having
their palm read.
So buy a book on
palmistry and foretell
your friends' futures.*

If you hear some great music when
you're in a bar or restaurant, don't be
embarrassed to ask what it is. Add it
to your playlist.

Miss the excitement of being in love? Then do something that will give you butterflies in your stomach: go on a rollercoaster, do a parachute jump or offer to make a speech at a social event.

If you're not happy in your job, it's time to update your CV and find one you'll love. Life's too short to do work you hate. Use your new 'me time' to work on yourself.

*Get involved in the local
community. It could be more
rewarding than you think. It's all
on your doorstep, after all. Read
the local paper and see what's
going on. There might be
musical or amateur dramatics
clubs that you can join, or a
local charity that could do with a
helping hand. Or you could set
up a group campaigning on local
environmental issues.*

Do something kind for someone without
them ever knowing. For example, for
someone whom you know is going through a
bad time, arrange a year's subscription to a
magazine that they like.

If you have a talent, share it! Pass on your skill to someone by becoming their teacher – it could be anything from learning how to use a computer to baking a cake.

Watch a thunderstorm at night – without being afraid to be alone.

Go to a live sporting event – perhaps a football, tennis or basketball match. You don't have to be a complete sports buff to enjoy yourself. Who knows, you might even get hooked.

Notice how many things you used to take for granted. Reacquaint yourself with the small pleasures in life. Go for a walk in the rain and splash in the puddles. Notice how fresh the air smells.

Stop thinking about doing something and make a start right now. What would you like to turn into a daily habit? It could be anything: doing 15 minutes of yoga sun salutations first thing in the morning, practising meditation, keeping a diary or running.

create a healthy,
happy you

Anyone who has been through a painful separation knows exactly how stressful this can be. It comes as no surprise then, that a split can be very detrimental to health. A number of studies suggest that the trauma of breaking up with a partner can lead to all sorts of health problems including migraines, skin problems, depression and insomnia – even heart disease. High stress levels suppress the immune system and this increases your risk of disease. But as long as you are aware of these factors there's no need to panic. Often, making the simplest lifestyle changes can help to safeguard your health.

Be yourself. Stop worrying about what you say and how you appear to others. By putting on a front and not expressing what you really think and feel, you are creating an imbalance of energy that will eventually erode your mental and physical health.

Run a marathon for charity. The training will improve your fitness level enormously, give you a new focus in life other than your relationship, and you'll feel so good knowing that the money raised is going to a good cause. Doing something worthwhile will also give you a profound sense of achievement.

Change your image and go shopping for some new clothes: maybe ones you wouldn't have bought when you were with your partner, because he or she wouldn't have liked them.

There may be moments when you miss your partner's caring touch. But there's no need to miss out completely. Experiment with simple feelgood massage techniques you can do for yourself. For example, it's very easy to give yourself a basic head massage, and it will make you feel good too. Using your fingertips, work over the surface of the scalp, the temples and the back of your head, applying pressure in circular movements. Pull gently at the roots of your hair, all over your head, to stimulate the hair follicles. Tap your scalp gently with a clenched fist. Apply pressure with one finger to the central point of your crown. Then apply pressure to the four points about 2.5cm/1in on each side of it (think north, south, east and west). These are the four calming points in shiatsu massage.

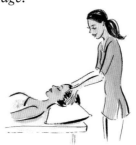

*Put the spring back in your step
with a revitalizing foot spa. Mix
essential oils – 2 drops of geranium
and 2 drops of orange – into a base
oil such as almond, and add to a
bowl of warm water. Soak your feet
for 5 to 10 minutes.*

There's no one else to lean on now. So, do what you can to maximize your energy. One way is to start each day with an invigorating sesame oil massage. This is a traditional energy tonic in the ancient Indian system of Ayurveda. Do it every morning before showering. The oil should be warmed in your hands first, then massaged briskly all over the body to energize the system and improve immunity.

If you've been burning the candle more than usual, go easy on those espressos. Research shows that in some people, drinking more than three cups of coffee a day can cause palpitations, trembling, irritability, sleeplessness and even panic attacks. So, if you don't want to feel jittery, try substituting mineral water, herbal teas, diluted fruit juices and grain coffees (made from chicory or barley).

Make sure you do some form of regular exercise every day, for at least 30 minutes, even if it's just going for a brisk walk. You can split the time into two sessions if it's easier. Exercise triggers the production of endorphins (feelgood chemicals in the brain). This helps to ward off depression, strengthens immunity and has an energizing effect.

Take up a holistic form of exercise such as tai chi, chi kung or yoga, all of which have both mental and physical benefits.

Spend a few minutes visualizing a happy event that you'd like to take place. It will make it more likely to come true.

With no partner to rush home to, it can be tempting to spend longer in the office. This could earn you a promotion. But all those long hours in front of the computer won't do your health much good. Research shows that computers and office equipment all emit invisible yet harmful pollutants. One simple way to protect yourself is to place green plants near computers, photocopiers, printers and faxes. Even a small cactus plant, for example, can help counteract the effects of radiation, and green plants generally can minimize the effects of pollutants such as formaldehyde, benzene and other chemicals from office machinery.

Make sure you're not at the bottom of the pile when it comes to asking for time off work. Don't let your employer take you for granted just because you're single. There's no need to feel guilty about making time for relaxing weekend breaks. Everyone should be able to have regular time out away from it all. And, even if you can't manage a week or a whole fortnight, make sure you take several mini-breaks to protect you from burn-out.

Rejuvenate with raw juice. Freshly made raw juices are nutritious, easy to digest, help cleanse and energize your system, and are packed with vitamins. So unearth that juicer you bought together but never used, and get blending apples, oranges, carrots, strawberries, celery and blueberries.

With no one to tempt you away from healthy eating, now's your chance to detox your diet. Clear your kitchen of all those sugar- and salt-laden processed foods and fill the shelves with nourishing wholegrain bread, pasta and rice, oats, nuts, fruits and vegetables.

> If you don't eat right and you don't know how to take care of your body, you're not going to have the energy to do anything wonderful.
>
> LOUISE L. HAY

If you're out and about a lot, carry small bags of nuts and seeds, or take some fruit to snack on. These are much healthier for you than biscuits, crisps and chocolate.

The next time you find yourself wallowing in nostalgia, or missing your ex, try some crystal therapy. Rose quartz, for example, has an uplifting, mind-calming effect. Aquamarine will help make you feel more balanced. Keep your chosen crystal near you for maximum effect.

Indulge yourself in a rosemary and salt bath if your muscles feel tired and ache after a hard day at work. Add 0.5kg/1lb Epsom salts to your bath, then sprinkle in a couple of drops of rosemary essential oil diluted with a base oil.

If you're having trouble sleeping, make a sleep pillow. Place some soothing dried herbs, such as lavender and camomile, in a small pillow and you will soon be deep in restful slumber.

Listen to a relaxation tape with recordings of natural sounds such as wind in the trees, waterfalls, birdsong. It may sound New Agey, but they do have a calming effect.

Feeling low? Turn up the volume and dance. Dancing reduces tension in the body and feelgood music makes the spirits soar.

Take a mood-boosting bath. Just add a few drops of uplifting essential oils such as grapefruit, neroli, mandarin, ginger, lemon or rose to the water. Always dilute them with a base oil such as jojoba, grapeseed or almond (1 drop essential oil per 5ml/1tsp base oil). The scent of essential oils acts upon the limbic (emotional) part of the brain.

Try an alternative therapy such as homoeopathy, reflexology, acupuncture or aromatherapy. This will help enhance your overall physical health and well-being.

Take the time to find new ways to make yourself feel good. For example, soak up the goodness of sea minerals by taking a thalassotherapy bath at home. Thalassotherapy is derived from the Greek word 'thalassa', which means 'sea'. Run a warm bath and add 50g (2oz) seaweed powder (available from health food shops) and 1 drop lavender essential oil, blended with1 tsp almond oil. Lie back for 20 minutes, and dream that you're floating under blue skies in the Aegean Sea.

Feeling agitated? Do the Cobra. This is a classic calming yoga move. Lie on the floor on your stomach with your hands under your shoulders, palms down. Then lift your body off the ground using your hands and arms, keeping your head up and back. Take several deep breaths while in this raised position. Slowly return to lying flat. Repeat four or five times.

Been throwing yourself into the single life with enthusiasm? Just make sure that all those late nights and parties don't mean you scrimp on sleep. Work out how many hours' sleep you need to feel refreshed (experts recommend seven) and make sure you get them. If you have trouble sleeping, avoid caffeine and alcohol in the few hours before you go to bed. Listen to a relaxation CD to help you nod off.

Be playful. Lighten up and have fun whenever you can.

Burn soothing essential oils such as frankincense, clary sage, bergamot, jasmine, rose and geranium to calm your mind if you're feeling down after a relationship split.

Fill your home with fresh flowers. Choose ones to suit your mood. For example, bright yellow daffodils or orange nasturtiums when you want to feel more energized, white arum lilies to create an aura of peace and calmness or delicate pink roses and peonies for a warm, happy atmosphere.

It's tempting to just graze haphazardly on food when you're on your own. But you need to eat regularly to keep your blood sugar levels stable throughout the day, and prevent those energy highs and lows that munching sugary or fatty snacks can cause.

If you've been burning the midnight oil at work, or even just having too many late nights partying, make sure you take time to rest and recuperate. Your body and mind need time to regenerate.

Make your surroundings even more special now that you're on your own. Light scented candles, surround yourself with beautiful objects and play calming background music.

Worried that all that recent relationship stress has gone to your waist? Learn to hula-hoop and whittle those spare inches away. It's much more fun than doing sit-ups.

After a break-up, stress and anxiety may manifest themselves in indigestion. Drink ginger tea to aid digestion. Just add a few slices of fresh ginger root, or a spoonful of dried ginger, to a cup of boiling water. Peppermint tea is also highly recommended.

You may be single now, but that doesn't mean you're relegated to ready meals for one, which often have minimal nutritional value and are packed with chemicals and additives. You deserve to cook delicious dinners for yourself.

If you suffer from phobias, depression and anxiety, don't suffer in silence. Think about seeing a qualified therapist or psychologist. If it is a mild case, you may be able to help yourself through relaxation techniques such as meditation, visualization or DIY hypnotherapy.

Treat yourself to a DVD of a movie you love, or a boxed set of a series or comedy that you enjoyed. Save it for when you're in exactly the right mood to hole up in front of the TV for an evening of indulgent viewing.

Exercise like mad the next time you feel anxious and hyper. When you're stressed, the body produces an excess of stress chemicals including cortisol and adrenaline. A build-up of these can lead to health problems; the best way to banish them is by doing vigorous exercise.

Make a fresh start and change your environment. You're on your own now. So, take this opportunity to create a healthier home. Invite plenty of natural light into your home and use natural materials such as wood, bamboo and wicker wherever possible.

> If only we'd stop trying to be happy we'd have a pretty good time.
> EDITH WHARTON

Your partner may have cleared out, but have you cleared your home of negative energies and emotions? For example, are there any rooms where you argued a lot, or where you felt sad and tense when you were a couple? You can purify and change a room's energy by burning candles or incense. Or burn a sage smudge stick to cleanse the atmosphere.

You're single now so you can be more flexible. Change is good for you and will help you to put things in perspective.

If waking up alone makes you feel low, here's something to pep you up first thing in the morning. Treat yourself to a fruit smoothie for breakfast. Spoon a small tub of low-fat yogurt into a blender, then add fruit such as bilberries, raspberries or strawberries, plus a banana and 50g/2oz powdered skimmed milk. The banana will help boost serotonin levels in your brain to keep depression at bay, and the milk and yogurt will ensure that you get at least half your recommended calcium intake for the day.

When one door of happiness closes, another opens. But often we look so long at the closed door that we do not see the one which has been opened for us.

HELEN KELLER

Don't let stress get on top of you. Let it all out in a way that works for you – go for a run, soak in a hot bath, meditate or thump a pillow.

Do a 'sacred space clearing'. This will help you reclaim your space as your own. You can cleanse the energy of a room with sound. One simple way to do this is to walk around the perimeter of the room and into the corners, clapping your hands loudly. The noise is thought to disperse negative and stagnant energy.

If you are feeling sad and lonely, carry a picture or photo around with you that makes you happy just looking at it – and look at it!

The next time you feel your body seize up with stress, try this simple strategy. Release tension in your neck and shoulders with a shoulder shrug. Just lift both shoulders to your ears, tighten them, then relax and let them drop down. Repeat a few times until you feel relaxed.

One of the simplest and quickest ways to calm yourself is to breathe slowly and deeply. This will increase your oxygen intake and your mind will feel calmer, yet physically you'll feel more energized.

Invest more energy in friends and activities that make you feel good.

You're on your own, so be responsible. Say what you mean – and mean what you say.

Now there's only you to shape your life. So take responsibility and stop blaming others.

> *Happiness belongs to the self-sufficient.*
> *ARISTOTLE*

Listen to music that makes you feel good.

Stop worrying about things you cannot control.

Take a walk on the wild side – along a windswept beach or a blustery clifftop.

Make the best of what you've got and focus on the good things in your life.

Don't let things wear you down. Stay young at heart and you'll look younger physically, too.

If you are a smoker, or tend to drink a lot when you are unhappy or stressed, keep a close watch on yourself to make sure that these habits don't intensify now. If you think your smoking or drinking is getting out of control, seek professional help and ideally try to give up altogether.

Learn a martial art. Knowing how to defend yourself physically will make you feel less vulnerable when you're out and about.

Make time to see your friends. You need them more than ever now.

Try to maintain a healthy weight. Comfort eating can soon lead to your clothes becoming uncomfortable. Remember: a moment on the lips, a lifetime on the hips …

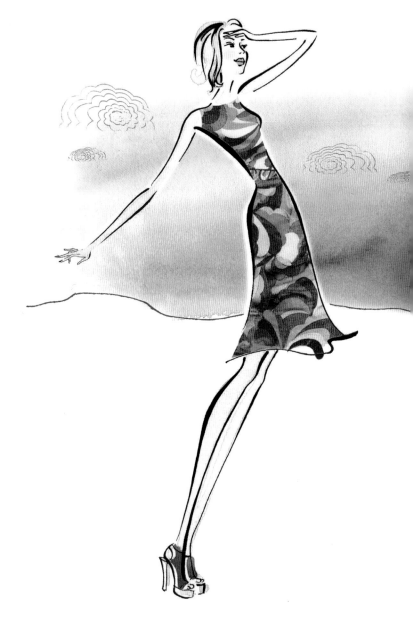

feed your
soul

It's only natural to become more introspective after a break-up. For many people, the end of a relationship can feel like the end of the world, especially if they've been married or living together for a long time. Suddenly, you're faced with all sorts of decisions and insecurities about your future. Where are you going to live? How will you manage financially? Will you ever meet anyone else? All these dilemmas come at a time when you're emotionally at your most vulnerable and stressed. It's at times like this that a little bit of soul sustenance can go a long way. Practices and rituals, such as meditation, for example – things that you might never have considered before – suddenly start to make sense. And, most importantly, help to you to heal and move on.

For mental clarity, meditate every day for 20 minutes. If your thinking is clear, bright and fresh, you'll be better equipped to come through the pain of a break-up and to face whatever the future might have in store. Meditating takes practice, so it might help to buy a book on the subject.

Alternatively, join a meditation group or class. This will deepen your spiritual awareness and you'll make some interesting new friends. As you develop spiritually, you will also find it easier to understand and let go of past traumas and issues relating to relationships.

If you find meditation hard, simply try to spend the 20 minutes a day in silence. Switch off your phone, TV, radio and computer and find a quiet place where you won't be disturbed. Close your eyes, relax your body, and let your mind wander. You'll be surprised how refreshed you feel afterwards.

If you are ever unsure about which path to take in life, or about making decisions, you need to learn to listen to your intuition, the small inner voice that tells you whether something feels right or not. Be still, go deep within to ask the questions, and listen for the answers.

Keep a diary and write down
all the good things that
happen to you every day.

Help someone out. One
upside of being single is that it
frees you to be more available
to help others.

> God doesn't look at how much we do, but with how much love we do it.
>
> MOTHER TERESA

Join a psychic development group. This can be very empowering as it will help you to develop an inner strength that you may never have known you had.

Think of a relaxing color, such as pale pink, lemon or lilac. Imagine yourself enveloped by this peaceful shade and feel how calm it makes you.

Read inspirational and uplifting books, especially those by people who have gone on to achieve amazing things in their lives after a relationship went wrong, or after some other trauma.

Look at every path closely and deliberately, then ask yourself this crucial question: does this path have a heart? If it does, then the path is good. If it doesn't, it is of no use.

CARLOS CASTANEDA

Protect yourself from negative energies by surrounding yourself with white light. Just visualize healing white light pouring into your body and forming a protective cocoon around you.

Keep your promises.

Stop mentally beating yourself up about mistakes you've made in the past. This includes whatever bad choices and decisions you feel you've made in relationships. Forgive yourself and move on.

Don't feel guilty if you have days when you just want to be on your own. Be grateful that you can be, and enjoy yourself.

Develop a world view beyond yourself. Volunteer to visit lonely, sick or old people in their homes or in hospital. You will gain from it as much as they do.

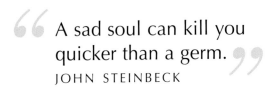

> A sad soul can kill you
> quicker than a germ.
> JOHN STEINBECK

An important way to move on from a past relationship is to get rid of anything that reminds you of the past, such as books and CDs you enjoyed together, the clothes you wore on your first date and photos from holidays.

Giving to others can help you to feel more purpose in your life. For example, donate a small amount of money, every month, to a charity that especially touches your heart.

If you're feeling sad about your situation, seek beyond yourself. Collect presents (get friends and colleagues involved as well) for homeless families and children's homes. Find out about these through your church or social services.

> *In order to experience everyday spirituality, we need to remember that we are spiritual beings spending some time in a human body.*
> BARBARA DE ANGELIS

You don't need a partner to go on a pilgrimage to a holy place. For example, visit Christian sites such as Santiago de Compostela, Lourdes, Iona, Canterbury and Glastonbury. Or travel to Mecca or the Ganges. Or discover ancient sacred sites such as Stonehenge, King Arthur's Castle in Tintagel, Machu Picchu, Ayers Rock and the Pyramids. Sacred sites are imbued with powerful, healing energies that can bring about a spiritual awakening.

He who has not looked on Sorrow will never see Joy.
KAHLIL GIBRAN

Being single means you have more scope to be reflective. Try to become more aware of your deepest thoughts. Acknowledge them and try to work out what they tell you about how you are really feeling.

We all have a spiritual purpose, a mission, that we have been pursuing without being fully aware of it, and once we bring it completely into consciousness, our lives can take off.
JAMES REDFIELD

Practise positive mantras daily. Take seven slips of paper, one for each day of the week, and write a positive message on each one. For example, 'I am able to achieve my goal', 'I am not afraid to face my fear' or 'Today is going to be wonderful'. Place each one in an envelope or little box and label it with a day. Each morning, take out the slip for that day and focus on the mantra for a few minutes before you start your day, repeating it out loud if that makes it more real for you.

Work out what your core beliefs and values are. These may have changed now that you are single.

Now that you're single again, ask yourself which activities satisfy you the most. Is it doing a job you enjoy, being creative, being with friends, visiting new destinations, learning new things or helping others? Find ways to spend more time doing those things.

> Make it a rule of life never to regret and never to look back. Regret is an appalling waste of energy; you can't build on it; it's only for wallowing in.
> KATHERINE MANSFIELD

A break-up can make you lose your emotional equilibrium temporarily. A few sessions of healing can help you feel whole again. The best way to find a reputable healer is through personal recommendation.

The truth is that our finest moments are most likely to occur when we are feeling deeply uncomfortable, unhappy, or unfulfilled. For it is only in such moments, propelled by our discomfort, that we are likely to step out of our ruts and start searching for different ways to truer answers.
M. SCOTT PECK

Instead of thinking 'Why me?', look at difficulties and challenges in your life as opportunities to grow, and take something positive from them.

Practise acceptance. Sometimes you just can't change things. So stop dwelling on what could be and try to be more accepting.

You might be single again, but be thankful for everything else that's good in your life. For example, the fact that you have good friends, a loving family, children, or a job you love.

Make time for a daily
spiritual ritual such as prayer,
or just taking time out to sit
quietly and reflect on your life.

Pay attention to your
dreams, emotions and
hunches – they might be
trying to tell you something.

Don't try and block out emotional pain. Face up to your feelings and don't let these numb you to future happiness. Emotional pain is often your spirit's way of letting you know that you need to make changes in your life.

Take joy in the small things in daily life: seeing a rainbow, having a cup of tea and a chat with a friend, stroking a pet, smelling a rose.

If you've got a problem and aren't sure how to deal with it, go with gut feeling and trust your intuition.

Does the prospect of being single terrify you? Think about taking a break from your everyday life and going on a spiritual retreat. The atmosphere, and the spiritual counsellors there, will help you face your fears and give you strength to conquer them.

Fears are more easily overcome by being brave and stepping out and doing the very thing we are afraid of, rather than waiting for our fear to go before trying something new.

If you're still feeling raw after a split, have a Reiki treatment. This is an ancient form of healing, which releases blocked energy and promotes a state of total relaxation. It stimulates the body's ability to heal itself and brings about spiritual, emotional and mental well-being.

Make a calming room spray by adding essential oils – 3 drops lavender, 2 drops jasmine, 2 drops palmarosa and 1 drop geranium – to a small spray bottle filled with mineral water. Shake to mix well and spray your home to create a peaceful atmosphere.

Do a healing Golden Light Meditation. This is a lovely meditation to do last thing at night before you go to bed. Imagine a ray of golden light streaming into your body. Focus on this energy for 10 to 15 minutes.

Wear a sapphire crystal to improve your intuition and open up your psychic abilities.

Feeling stressed? Take a Dead Sea salt bath at the end of the day to cleanse your aura. Just add a handful of sea salts (available from health food shops) to a hot bath and soak for about 10 to 15 minutes.

The next time you have a wonderful holiday, bring back a CD of music you heard at the time. Whenever you play it at home, it will remind you of what a good time you had and flood you with happy feelings.

Gather like-minded friends together for a full moon meditation, or go for a moonlit walk.

Negative self-chatter can really drag you down. So override those nagging voices telling you're no good, or fat, or will never find love again, with positive voices saying you're gorgeous, popular and can do anything.

Flower therapy can have you blooming again. Consult a flower essence practitioner to find out what essences you need to bring about emotional and physical healing. For example, Star of Bethlehem is useful for feelings of grief and loss; Honeysuckle can help you move on if you keep going over old ground and are stuck in the past; Larch can help you feel more confident; Sweet Chestnut can help you regain optimism.

Do you feel you have had the stuffing knocked out of you by a tempestuous break-up? An effective way to regain strength is to work on your chakras through alternative therapies. In Eastern thought, chakras are seven main energy sites (spinning wheels of energy in the body, located along the 'energetic' spine). Each major chakra is associated with different organs, glands, emotions, characteristics and colors. When chakras are out of balance, it affects your emotional, mental and physical well-being. When they are spinning equally, energy is vibrating at exactly the right level and you feel great.

Forgive anyone who has hurt you — including your ex — you'll feel better for it.

Accept that you are single right now for a reason. Perhaps you need this time alone to grow spiritually. Trust that you will meet the right person when the time is right.

Create a scrapbook that contains positive photos, affirmations, quotations, poems and so on, which reflect all the good things you want to achieve or attract into your life. For example, if you'd like to run a marathon, stick in a picture of Paula Radcliffe. Looking at your scrapbook will help you to focus on and visualize your goals.

Don't underestimate the power of the mind. You can achieve miracles if you put your mind to it.

You won't always get what you 'want' but you will always get what you 'need' to help you grow spiritually. This includes relationships.

Practise qigong. This is a gentle, ancient Chinese mind and body exercise that has both emotional and physical benefits.

The dark night of the soul comes just before revelation.
JOSEPH CAMPBELL

Get a pack of Angel cards—each card contains an affirmation from different angels. Each day choose a new card, read what it says and let that be your inspiration for the day.

Burn sandalwood incense sticks to clear negative energies from your surroundings.

Learn the art of divination by using a simple divination tool such as the Runes or the I Ching. See what changes you can predict in your love life.

You never have to do anything. Don't know what to do? Do nothing. I wait. And that has been a big lesson: to be willing, to be still with myself, and trust myself and my higher power to help me make the right decision. And to not feel pressured.
OPRAH WINFREY

Think of heartbreak as an opportunity to open your heart. Going through a bad time emotionally may feel terrible at the time, but it will make you more able to empathize and understand others when they are suffering in any way.

Feeling hyper? Here's an easy way to calm down. Close your eyes, take a deep breath and relax. Now, imagine yourself floating on your back in a sea of aquamarine water, looking up at a turquoise sky. Meditating on the anything blue is very uplifting. It helps reduce blood pressure, calms brainwave activity and lowers the heart rate.

A great way to take your mind off your worries is to think of others. Do what you can to help others to achieve their goals and dreams.

rediscover
your zing

The first few weeks after you've split up with someone can be a bit daunting. You may also find that your energy levels are lower than usual. That's when you need to nurture your body and find the best ways to energize yourself when you're feeling low. This could mean rethinking your diet, your exercise regime, or the clothes you wear. The good news is that there are lots of simple things you can do, on a daily basis, make yourself feel better and more full of zest.

Use a grapefruit or lime shower gel in the morning, as the fresh scent will give you zest for the day ahead.

There's nothing to stop you – and no one to tease you – if you want to do 100 sit-ups or run round the block. A burst of movement can boost your energy brilliantly.

Drink a glass of hot water with freshly squeezed lemon juice first thing in the morning, to purify your system and skin. Lemon stimulates the liver to work properly, and when your liver is working well, you have more energy.

Make the extra effort to prepare a fruit salad. Throw in fresh pineapple, strawberries, grapefruit, tangerine segments, cranberries and grapes, all of which are packed with powerful antioxidants and masses of revitalizing vitamin C.

Emotional upheavals can really knock your energy levels, but a few simple dietary changes can help. The best energy booster is to have a nutritious breakfast to set you up for the day. Porridge is perfect, as the sustained energy provided by oats prevents your blood sugar dipping and making you reach for a mid-morning doughnut. Other excellent choices which combine complex carbs with protein, are scrambled or poached eggs on wholemeal toast, and yogurt sprinkled with berries or dried fruit, nuts and seeds.

Tidy up. According to the principles of the ancient Chinese art of feng shui, clutter blocks energy flow. And, depending on which area or areas of your home it is in, it will affect your prospects of happiness and good fortune. For example, if you're single, you may find it difficult to meet someone. Moving your bed or a mirror can also attract good things into your life. Whether you believe in feng shui or not, it's only common sense that life will be easier if your home is neat. For one thing, you won't waste hours searching for your car keys or that important bill.

If you feel sluggish, eat foods that cleanse your liver and help eliminate toxins, such as beetroot, cucumber, apple, onions, garlic and pears. Milk thistle supplements can also help.

Choose your colors with care, as they can have a powerful effect on your mood and well-being. Soft yellows, pinks, creams and terracotta are high on the feelgood factor. Green is obviously aligned with nature and is very calming. Orange is good for dining areas, because it stimulates the appetite. Red is a great passion enhancer, so is ideal for the bedroom if you want to attract love into your life. Shades of blue are restful and so can promote restorative sleep.

Make showering more invigorating with an all-over Dead Sea salt massage beforehand. Make up a paste of coarse sea salt (available in health food shops) mixed with warm water. Massage it in a circular motion all over your body with your hands or a sisal friction mitt. The brisk massage helps boost circulation, sloughs off dead skin and really wakes you up. Shower off afterwards.

Take care to spend at least an hour a day outdoors. A daily dose of sunlight can work wonders for your mood, and research shows that not getting enough natural light can lead to depression, irritability, insomnia and fatigue.

Take in the scent of fresh green apple for an energizing effect.

Have an invigorating bath in the morning by blending 3 to 6 drops of energizing essential oils, such as rosemary, lemon, peppermint or grapefruit, with a base oil such as grapeseed or jojoba (1 drop essential oil to 5ml (1 tsp) base oil) and adding it to your bath.

Pamper yourself with soft, clean and soothing bedlinen. Choose Egyptian cotton sheets and huge plump pillows.

Rather than meeting friends indoors, arrange to go for a walk in the woods, sit by the river or spend time in a beautiful park. Aligning yourself with nature brings your body back into its natural rhythm. Your brainwaves go into relaxing alpha wave mode and you breathe more deeply, so energy flows more freely throughout your body.

With no one around to distract you, make resolutions that you know you'll stick to. These can be anything from going to the gym to seeing friends more often.

Do something every day that makes you laugh. Meet or talk to a friend who gets you giggling. Exchange funny e-mails, read a book that makes you laugh out loud, or watch a comedy programme. Notice how energized and good you feel afterwards. Laughter relaxes muscle tension, soothes nerves, lowers high blood pressure and helps boost the immune system.

Sweat out your worries and tensions in a sauna or steam room. It's a great way to get rid of toxins and cleanse your system.

Whenever you're tempted to feel sorry for yourself, get physical. Dance around the room to a CD, go for a ride, head to the gym or have a swim. A good workout – even just half an hour – can boost your levels of feelgood serotonin and endorphins.

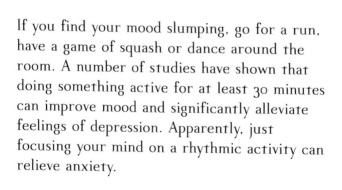

If you find your mood slumping, go for a run, have a game of squash or dance around the room. A number of studies have shown that doing something active for at least 30 minutes can improve mood and significantly alleviate feelings of depression. Apparently, just focusing your mind on a rhythmic activity can relieve anxiety.

Try to identify what drains and depletes your energy and try to avoid those situations and people.

If you're lacking in energy and want an instant boost – red will make you feel more zingy. So, put on some red clothes, use a red light bulb, or just stare at a red painting. Red is stimulating and gets the circulation going.

Regularly drinking more water regularly will instantly improve your energy levels and concentration, as well as your skin. Ideally, you should drink about 2 litres (3½ pints) a day. That's about eight glasses of water. Don't worry if you find that too hard – diluted fruit juice and herbal teas can count towards the total. The body actually finds it easier to absorb water when it is mixed with another liquid.

Wear orange if you are depressed or your self-esteem is low. Orange can help you to feel better about yourself. It attracts joy into your life.

The next time you're going out and want to look and feel your best, give yourself a DIY acupressure facial massage beforehand. This will stimulate your circulation and leave you feeling renewed, refreshed and clear-headed. Place the index and middle fingers of both hands in the middle of your forehead and smooth them outwards towards the temples. Using a light massaging motion, circle the temples with your fingertips. Then gently rub your cheeks in a circular motion. Rub the end of your nose and pinch along the lower jaw. Finally, pull your ears up, down and forward.

If you're feeling down, beat the blues with a mood-lifting lemon balm tea. Put 30g/1¼oz fresh lemon balm leaves in a teapot and add 600ml/1 pint of boiling water. Steep for 10 minutes before drinking.

It may be chic, classic and slimming, and the fashionista's uniform, but wearing black head to toe every day can be depressing. If you can't manage a pink shirt or blue skirt to lighten your mood, try something different in your accessories – maybe a pair of red shoes or an apple green scarf.

Arrange to go to a health spa with friends for a day or a weekend.

Have a holistic, therapeutic or sports massage regularly.

Transform your bathroom into a home spa for the day. Light some candles and put soothing ambient sounds on the CD player.

Don't let yourself go just because there's no one to hold hands with right now. Treat yourself to a manicure.

Exfoliate skin daily with a dry body brush to boost circulation, keep cellulite at bay, and strengthen immunity.

One joy of being single is that there's no one to bang on the bathroom door when you're doing a beauty treatments. So give yourself a facial once a week.

Feel like you haven't had enough sleep? Have a hot shower, followed at once by a cold one. This really gets the circulation going and will instantly make you feel much more alert.

Go heels over head to recharge your batteries. Lie down and raise your legs over your head. Support yourself with your hands on your hips. Hold for 1–2 minutes.

After an exhausting day at work, call in at a health club or beauty salon on the way home for a relaxing neck and shoulder massage.

Take a tip from your pet cat and try the Cat yoga position to revive your energy. Get down on all fours, head looking downwards, hips aligned with knees and shoulders, and hands palm down on the ground. Slowly raise your back into a cat-like curve. Hold for a few seconds, then slowly raise your head and allow your back to dip. Repeat three or four times.

Breaking up with a partner is stressful, no matter who instigated the split. Taking a course of supplements can help prevent you from becoming run down. Stress depletes vitamins and minerals, especially vitamins B and C. So take a good multivitamin and mineral supplement daily.

Natural daylight is a great mood booster. A good way to make sure you're getting enough is to use natural daylight bulbs at home.

Does the thought of your ex sometimes make you hyperventilate? The next time this happens, sit down and stretch your arms out wide. Breathe slowly and deeply in and out (into a paper bag if it helps) until you feel your abdominal area loosen up. Nervous tension gathers in the abdominal region, so anything that relaxes this area will help.

Break old habits in more ways than one and make new health resolutions. For example, drink delicious herbal teas, such as peppermint or zesty orange and blackcurrant, instead of energy-zapping processed fruit juices, fizzy drinks and coffee.

Do you dive into the biscuit tin when you're feeling down? Munch energy-giving oatcakes instead. Oats help stabilize blood sugar levels and keep you feeling full for longer.

Some people lose weight when they split up with a partner, others pile it on. Neither is good for you. So, make sure you eat regularly and sensibly, even if it's the last thing you feel like doing.

Take some form of living food supplement such as wheatgrass, chlorella or spirulina. These are packed with health giving goodness in a highly digestible, living form.

Don't crash-diet, telling yourself your ex wouldn't have left had you been thinner. A weight change of more than 20 per cent in two years puts strain on the body, increasing the risk of high blood pressure, heart attack and kidney problems.

Can't face the gym? Perhaps jogging round the block seems too much like hard work. Make exercise more fun: buy a skipping rope and skip for exercise.

Drink green tea as well as black, as it contains several powerful antioxidants that are highly beneficial to health.

Break ties with a former partner by doing this healing visualization. Imagine standing next to your ex. Now picture a beautiful blue light separating you both. Focus on this flowing, healing light for a few minutes. Imagine pouring all your anger and frustration into it, and watch how the cooling blue disperses your red-hot anger and resentment. Stay like this until you start to feel peaceful and forgiving towards your partner.

Do something different. Make yourself feel good and adorn your home with plants. The more beautiful and unusual the better. Think tropical or Venus flytrap rather than run-of-the-mill spider plants and ferns.

Protect yourself against depression with a tablespoonful of sunflower, pumpkin, sesame or linseeds every day. These are rich in essential fatty acids (omega-3 and omega-6) which have been found to be low in people suffering from depression. Eating two portions of oily fish a week, or taking cod liver oil or other omega-3 and omega-6 supplements is also recommended.

Surround yourself with scents that remind you of happy times in your life. For example, a gorgeous fragrance, soap or essential oil that you bought on a wonderful holiday, or that you used as a child. Every time you smell it, you'll be transported back to that happy time.

Had a late night? Wake yourself up by splashing freezing cold water on your face, or spend 10 minutes running vigorously on the spot.

Have a gym workout for a rosy glow. Exercise stimulates your circulation and works wonders for your complexion.

Keep yourself perky for the evening by taking a power nap during the day. Top executives do it!

*think creatively
and act
confidently*

It might not feel like it right now, but breaking up could be the best thing that's ever happened to you. Often, it's only when you hit rock bottom emotionally that you start to access your true strengths and talents. Challenges and obstacles are the greatest teachers. Difficult situations force us to look deep inside and discover what we're made of. Just think of all the great poems and songs that have resulted from heartbreak. A break up can make you feel more insular and detached for a while. Often, this is exactly the mindset you need to inspire you to experiment with your creativity. Decide that it's time to build up your confidence.

Vamp it up! Add glitter to your life and personalize a plain T-shirt with sequins.

Express your creativity and surprise a friend with a beautiful handmade birthday card.

" A hunch is creativity trying to tell you something. "
ANON

Awaken the designer within.
Buy some gorgeous fabric and
design a unique dress or top.

Take acting classes. You don't have to want to be an actor to benefit. Improving the way you speak, move, hold yourself and generally come across can also work wonders in your work and social life.

Ditch your professional, dull-as-ditchwater business cards and create some exciting new ones.

Carry a notebook around with you so that the new, creative you can jot down any interesting thoughts, ideas and observations whenever they come.

"It is better to have enough ideas for some to be wrong, than to always be right by having no ideas at all. "
EDWARD DE BONO

Fancy yourself as a scriptwriter? Think of a plot and visualize all the different characters. Write a short scene every day. When it's finished, send a synopsis to a TV company and see what happens.

Write a poem about your best friend. It doesn't matter if it's more of ditty than a sonnet. The fact that you've made the effort is what matters.

" Imagination is more important than knowledge. For while knowledge defines all we currently know and understand, imagination points to all we might yet discover and create. "
ALBERT EINSTEIN

The next time a good friend has a milestone birthday, gets married or celebrates a special occasion, take a Polaroid camera to the party, take lots of photos and then compile a scrapbook for him or her complete with messages, captions and comments from other guests. It will be a permanent keepsake from a special day.

Now that you're free of all ties, there's nothing to stop you following your dreams. So if you've always secretly wanted to be a rock star, now's your chance. Instead of wasting precious hours moping in front of the TV, make up for lost time and learn to play the drums, or strum a few tunes on a guitar.

Have singing lessons. Even if your voice is close in pitch to the cat next door, that's not the issue. There's something incredibly uplifting about belting out a good song, and it's been proved to improve your mood and lung capacity.

Put some of that spare time to good use and learn to give a really good massage. It might come in handy next time you meet someone special!

Create some unique postcards of all your friends. Spend a day or two taking photographs. Try to get some original shots and get them printed up as postcards you can send.

Learn to play a few songs on the piano or guitar, so you can surprise friends with an impromptu party piece.

Want to know if your love life is going to improve? Learn to read tarot cards. You never know what the cards will reveal.

Don't let a love split affect your confidence. Spend a few minutes every day thinking back over all the things you've done well in the past. It could be anything: passing your driving test, giving a brilliant presentation at work, throwing a fantastic party, or helping a friend who was in trouble.

Write down a list of all your positive attributes and remind yourself of them whenever you feel you're not good enough.

When you come out of a relationship it is a good time to look at old patterns and behaviours. Things can be different next time round. Decide what your boundaries are and stand up for yourself if you feel they're being broken. For example, if you don't like the rude, offhand way in which someone speaks to you, be assertive and let them know in a calm, firm, courteous manner. Ultimately, people will treat you the way you allow yourself to be treated.

You may be single, but make an effort with your appearance every day, even if you don't feel like it.

Smile. It's a well-established psychological fact that if you act in a certain way, the brain soon follows. Not convinced? The next time you feel low because you miss your ex, stand in front of the mirror and smile. You'll find it's impossible to feel down with a smile on your lips. According to psychologists, a turned-up mouth changes the facial muscles and sends a message to the brain that has a feelgood effect.

Keep a dream journal. Tuning in to your dreams can help enhance creativity. Dreams can also bring to light potential problem areas in your life that you may not be fully aware of. For example, you may still have some unresolved issues to do with past relationships. Looking to your dreams for insight can be a useful psychological tool for helping you to move on. Keep a pen and notebook beside your bed. The moment you wake up, write down your dreams. Make a note of images and any feelings you had. A book on the interpretation of dreams will help you uncover what your dreams may mean.

If you want to feel more mentally alert, wear yellow. Or paint your surroundings in primrose or buttercup. Yellow stimulates the mind and enhances learning and creative thinking, as well as being uplifting.

> When we create something, we always create it first in a thought form. If we are basically positive in attitude, expecting and envisioning pleasure, satisfaction and happiness, we will attract and create people, situations, and events which conform to our positive expectations.
>
> SHAKTI GAWAIN

Not sure what to do about a certain situation or problem? Then take a piece of paper and write a list of solutions. This will help you to see your options better. There's never just one answer.

Few things can boost your confidence like a fabulous new hairstyle: not just a timid trim, but a dramatic new cut or hairdye. A happy, bouncy new you will waltz out of the salon and you'll soon be glowing with all the compliments you'll receive.

If you are lacking in confidence, red will help you feel more sure of yourself. Wearing red will help boost feelings of courage, strength and vitality. It will also make you feel more grounded. So splash out on those scarlet stilettos.

Pay attention to the way you speak, especially if you want to impress a new admirer. Nerves can make you gabble like a Grand Prix commentator, which can be offputting. So put the brakes on and slow down.

Wear something turquoise if you want to bring out your creativity. Turquoise signifies intuitive creative expression. It will also help you to be more eloquent, so wear it if you need to speak at a meeting or presentation.

Sometimes you've got to let everything go – purge yourself. If you are unhappy with anything . . . whatever is bringing you down, get rid of it. Because you'll find that when you're free, your true creativity, your true self comes out.
TINA TURNER

Make yourself more attractive by emanating a positive energy. You can work on this by feeding your mind with positive ideas, thoughts and inspirations.

Don't dwell on what went wrong. Focus on past successes instead. That includes good relationships too.

Next time you get stuck in a creative rut, get moving. Exercise boosts blood circulation to the brain and gets the creative juices flowing.

Your budget might not stretch to a new purchase, but you can still breathe life into an outfit, bag or pair of shoes by dyeing it a different color.

Every time you focus on some part of your body or personality that you're unhappy with, substitute something that you are happy with. For example, instead of dwelling on your fat thighs, think about what beautiful blue eyes you've got. Instead of thinking you can't tell a joke, remind yourself of what a good listener you are.

Enlarge photos you love, frame them and hang them up on your walls at home.

Give people the space to be themselves. People can sense if you expect them to act in a certain way. This can make you come across as needy and controlling, and will have people backing off in record time.

" One of our greatest gifts is our intuition. It is a sixth sense we all have – we just need to learn to tap into and trust it. "

DONNA KARAN

Develop your talents. Not sure what these are? Then ask a good friend to remind you.

You may feel like a gibbering wreck socially, but the trick is not to show it. Learn to manage your anxiety. If you can remain calm and unflustered, you will automatically appear more confident. Acting confidently will also boost your appeal and make you more attractive to potential new admirers.

To appear confident and self-assured, be aware of non-verbal tics that could be scuppering your chances of escaping being a singleton. For example, slouching as you walk, not making eye contact, fidgeting, twitching or playing with your hair.

Creativity is inventing, experimenting, growing, taking risks, breaking rules, making mistakes and having fun.
MARY LOU COOK

> *One important key to success is self-confidence. An important key to self-confidence is preparation.*
>
> ARTHUR ASHE

Ask friends to tell you what they like about you, or what you do well.

If you lack confidence in certain areas, such as sport or computer skills, take classes that will help you to become more competent. Your new confidence will spill over into other areas of your life.

Take action. The more proactive you are, the more confident you will feel. Don't just sit there waiting for things to happen. If you want to meet a new partner, or expand your social circle, you need to get out of your comfort zone.

> Creativity involves breaking out of established patterns in order to look at things in a different way.
> EDWARD DE BONO

Still feeling bad about breaking up with your ex? Why not write a song or poem about how you feel? It's a great way to get things off your chest and tap into your creativity. Or listen to songs by singers that were inspired by their own break-ups (as many have been); it will help you understand that you're not alone, and that others have felt just as you are feeling now.

Make sure you are prepared for challenging situations. The more you plan ahead, the more confident you will feel about handling whatever comes your way.

Keep a doodle pad and notice how your doodles change depending on your mood. Like dreams, doodles can help you to get in touch with your inner self.

Try some crystal therapy. Wear or carry citrine or rose quartz to boost self-confidence, and lapis lazuli to enhance creativity.

Don't let a bad relationship rock your confidence. Take an assertiveness course and feel more empowered.

Keep a file where you can store pictures, photos and cuttings from magazines and newspapers which inspire you.

Revel in your single status – enjoy the freedom, and the opportunity to be totally yourself and to develop your life and talents in whatever direction you want.

Don't wait until everything is just right. It will never be perfect. There will always be challenges, obstacles and less than perfect conditions. So what. Get started now. With each step you take, you will grow stronger and stronger, more and more skilled, more and more self-confident and more and more successful.
MARK VICTOR HANSEN

Take the focus off yourself. Be genuinely interested in other people. Notice what's important to them, and what mood they're in.

rethink your
relationships

One of the biggest bonuses of coming out of a relationship is that it frees you up to engage more fully with other people. Let's face it, even the best relationships take up emotional energy. This means you have less time, or incentive, to put energy into other friendships. But now's your chance to make up for lost time. You're free to make new friends, to enjoy existing friendships, to spend more time with family, and to reflect on your core values and what it is you really want.

Spend more time with people who inspire you and make you feel great. Avoid anyone who puts you down and has a draining effect.

Accept that when a relationship breaks down, this may cause inevitable changes in your social life. Don't be scared to let go of friendships that aren't working any more.

You may love your friends and family – but how often do you show it? Take time to make them feel appreciated. You'll be surprised how much calmer and happier this will make you feel.

You might not feel like socializing much right now, but good friendships are essential for your well-being. Being single again makes us realize how much friends mean to us. If you find it difficult to make new friends, it could be that your self-esteem is low.

Making friends is a matter of confidence. If you like yourself, others will be attracted to you. If you feel your confidence needs building up, a good way to do this is to learn something new – take up a sport or study a subject you enjoy. Discovering a hidden talent can work wonders for boosting self-esteem.

If you've recently moved house, make an effort to get to know your new neighbours. They could become good friends, who'll help you when you lock yourself out and keep an eye on your home when you're away on holiday. And you can do the same for them. They may introduce you to their friends, one of whom may prove to be that special someone.

> *Everything that irritates us about others can lead us to an understanding of ourselves.*
> CARL JUNG

Treat others as you would like to be treated. It sounds obvious, but it's easy to forget. If you feel good about yourself, you're more likely to treat others with compassion, understanding and consideration.

If your split-up wasn't amicable, try not to feel bitter. One bad experience doesn't mean everyone's out to get you. Look for the good in others.

It's better to trust until you're let down, rather than to be naturally suspicious. If you're always expecting the worst, you'll miss out on much joy.

Really listen to what people have to say. This makes them feel special and shows you are interested in them. Most people love being with those who make them feel special.

> We can increase the frequency of guiding coincidences by uplifting every person that comes into our lives. Care must be taken not to lose our inner connection in romantic relationships.
>
> JAMES REDFIELD

Cultivate a variety of different friendships. It's healthy and stimulating to have friends or groups of friends that are different. That way, you can express different parts of your personality. Some friends may be brilliant to go out with and have a laugh with, but not so good at mulling over the meaning of life whilst sharing a bottle of wine, or helping in a crisis. Mixing with different types of people brings balance and fulfilment to your life.

Get back in the loop. Practise your social skills by talking to people at bus stops, in shops and at the gym.

If you've recently been through a traumatic time yourself, you'll know just how much a friend can help with getting you to smile again. So the next time a friend is in trouble, you'll be the perfect person to console, support and cheer her.

You can never really change others, so don't try. Change yourself instead.

If someone does something to make your blood boil, breathe deeply and think of three things you like about them.

Don't let the ghost of a past bad relationship haunt you. That was then – and now it really is up to you to move on. Choose the way you feel. Nobody can 'make' you feel bad – unless you let them.

" The things our friends do with us and for us form a portion of our lives, they strengthen our personality. "
JOHANN WOLFGANG VON GOETHE

Be supportive, but don't always try to bail people out of their problems. Sometimes people have to work things out for themselves and it helps them to become stronger.

Now that you're single, take pleasure in meeting all sorts of different people whom you might not have had time to socialize with before.

Life won't go smoothly all the time, but try to keep your sense of humour.

Now you're on your own, you don't have to socialize with people you don't really like just to keep your partner happy. So be selective. Only spend time with people you really want to see.

"**People who cannot be friends cannot make friends.**"
WILLIAM HAZLITT

Don't feel you always have to have the last word. No one likes a smart Alec.

Just because you're single now, there's no need to compromise with making new friendships because you're feeling a bit lonely. Be discriminating.

Don't be scared to let certain friendships go. If someone is always letting you down, being ultra-critical and just generally taking you for granted, cut your losses and let them go.

Keep a stash of pretty cards to send as thank-you notes after a party or visit. It's only courteous, and the guests who take the trouble to say thank you for all the effort their hosts went to, and say how much they enjoyed themselves, are the ones who'll be invited again.

You might not be feeling on top of the world, but be happy for your friends when something good happens in their lives.

" It is the enemy who can truly teach us to practise the virtues of compassion and tolerance. "

DALAI LAMA

A good friend is one who gives a kind of happiness based on knowing interconnectedness; learning to be friends to ourselves and being one to others.
THE BUDDHA

Give more . . . and expect less.

Remember that moods are contagious. So even if you feel like moaning, try not to. Be positive instead. Why bring people down when you can choose to brighten everyone's day?

Instead of waiting for someone to ask you out, make the first move yourself. If you want to get to know someone better, invite him or her for coffee, or a drink, or to see a film with you. What have you got to lose?

Pay attention to significant occasions in your friends' lives. Make a note of birthdays and anniversaries, and also of worrying events such as a hospital appointment or the day of scan results. Let them know you are thinking about them. Send a card, call them or offer to be with them.

Partners come and go, but good friends are worth their weight in gold. Let your friends know how much they mean to you. Everyone loves to be appreciated.

A relationship is an initiation, in a way. As you work things out, you actually become a more mature person. That's a very good way in which a relationship serves your soul.
THOMAS MORE

It doesn't matter if it's an old friend, or a hot new date – always try to bring out the best in people.

Instead of complaining that you never meet anyone special, it could be that you're not giving people a chance. Assume that everyone has something interesting about them. It's up to you to find out what it is.

If you're finding it difficult to get on with someone, try to put yourself in their shoes. It could help you understand them better and work out why they're acting in a certain way.

Make sure you don't turn friends into a surrogate partner now that you're single. And, on the same note, don't expect one friend to fulfil all your needs. Your partner didn't! Appreciate that each friend offers something unique.

Don't be too possessive. Give friends (and potential new partners) space and expect it yourself. There's nothing more offputting than a clingy, cloying friend who demands to know what you're up to every minute of the day. And who sulks when you won't see them all the time.

Notice how good you feel when you can be totally yourself with certain people. When you can tell them about your day and they really listen. When you can have an off day and they understand. They like you for who you are. This works both ways. So accept friends for who they are.

Just like some partners, accept that some friends are only ever meant to come into your life for a short time.

Curb the urge to give out unsolicited advice. Sometimes friends just want to get things off their chest without needing or wanting you to go into full-blown life coach or counsellor mode. The same applies to first dates. The idea is to have fun and get to know each other. If you turn it into a life-coaching session, you may wave goodbye to romance.

> Go through your phone book, call people and ask them to drive you to the airport. The ones who will drive you are your true friends. The rest aren't bad people; they're just acquaintances.
>
> JAY LENO

If a friend asks you to keep a secret, do so.

Do what you can to cheer up a friend when they're feeling down. Let them talk, try and make them laugh, buy them some flowers, a silly card or suggest a fun activity that will help them to switch off from their problems.

Don't be too accommodating. While there's nothing wrong with being a supportive, caring friend, you also need to have certain boundaries. The same goes for new partners – don't be too eager, too soon. Make them earn your goodwill. People will respect you more that way.

" A friend is one to whom one may pour out all the contents of one's heart, chaff and grain together, knowing that the gentlest of hands will take and sift it, keep what is worth keeping and with a breath of kindness blow the rest away. "

ARABIAN PROVERB

Don't let good friendships fall apart just because you live miles apart – or in other countries. E-mail, send cards and texts, and make regular phone calls.

Stand up for your friends if someone is putting them down. Apply the same criteria to new partners. Think about making a run for it if they put their friends down. They're hardly going to be loyal to you.

Are you the person everyone always turns to when they have a problem? That's great, as it proves you're a caring, trustworthy and sensitive person. But make sure it's not all one-sided. Don't be afraid to ask for advice and help when you need it.

Don't wait for others to arrange social events. Organize group activities that will enable people to get to know each other.

> You can make more friends in two months by becoming interested in other people than you can in two years by trying to get other people interested in you.
>
> DALE CARNEGIE

Nervous about a new date? You might not be the only one. Recognize when someone is shy and help them come out of their shell. You'll be so focused on doing it that you'll forget to be shy yourself!

Want to know how to keep those social invites and dates flooding in? Be a good listener. Ask people their opinions and get them to talk about subjects they love.

Widening your social circle is a good way to meet a new partner. You never know, your new friends might know someone who's perfect for you.

Don't be scared to speak your mind sometimes. Friendship doesn't mean you have to agree about everything. True friendship can take honesty, if it's expressed thoughtfully and kindly.

No matter what good friends you are – people aren't mind-readers. So, if someone has done something to upset you, let them know rather than make them guess. At least that way there's more chance you can put things right.

Be encouraging and positive when friends tell you their dreams and plans.

Don't be too proud to say sorry.

Be trustworthy.
A friendship is
nothing without trust.

Friendship is certainly the finest balm
for the pangs of disappointed love.
JANE AUSTEN

If you really can't stand someone, rather than focusing on why they annoy you so much, send them love instead.

trying again/
finding new love

Everyone reacts differently when they split up with their partner. Some people feel like crawling into a corner to lick their wounds and vow they'll never let anyone get that close again. Others can't wait to get out there and meet as many new people as possible in an attempt to heal their pain. Eventually, for most people, there comes a point when they're keen to meet someone special again. But if you've been with someone for a long time, you may feel as if you've forgotten what to do, where to go and how to act. If that sounds like you, here are a few guidelines to get you back into the swing of things. If you follow these suggestions, you'll be dating before you know it.

Take up a sport that's popular with the opposite sex. For example, if you're a woman, learn to play golf or join your local squash club. If you're a man, join a yoga or dance class, or brush up on your tennis skills.

Become a volunteer. Keep an eye out (look in the local newspaper) for organizations that need a helping hand. For example, you might spot opportunities for helping out in a hospital, church or shelter for the homeless. This will not only make you feel good, because you're doing something worthwhile, but you'll also increase your chances of locking eyes with an attractive, caring stranger.

Get involved in local politics. Contact your local council and find out about meetings in your area. Party volunteers are always in high demand and you're bound to find yourself in some lively debate

The next time there's a big sporting event, don't hole up at home with a beer and hot dog. Get down to the nearest pub or bar where there's a lively crowd watching it on TV. You'll all have something in common, so it'll be much easier to strike up casual friendly banter. It could prove the perfect match in more ways than one ...

Go back to college. Even if you only enrol on a part-time, one-evening-a-week computer, counselling or language course, you'll be entitled to use all the facilities. That means the student bar and library, not to mention access to all sorts of social events, where you're bound to meet other like-minded types of all ages.

Even if you have a top-of-the-range washing machine, try hanging out at your local launderette occasionally.

Keep tabs on any interesting events at your local bookshops or library, such as author signings, book launches or book readings. You'll meet lots of fellow bookworms.

Be open-minded. Even if you think they're not for you, try events such as speed dating or singles nights, at your local bar or nightclub, at least once. You may find you enjoy them, even if you don't meet your soulmate. Ask a single friend to go with you if you're nervous.

Join a sports club or gym. As well as getting fit, you could find yourself next to a handsome hunk or gorgeous girl as you pedal away on your exercise bike.

Attend a convention for something you're interested in such as astrology, glam rock, vintage cars or motor bikes.

Many couples meet at work. But that's hard to do if there's no one vaguely fanciable in your office. So take a part-time job that involves contact with lots of new people. For example, waitressing, bar work, or selling on a market stall.

Act more confidently than you feel.
It doesn't matter if you're not a raving
beauty or hot-looking guy. Acting
confidently will boost your appeal.

Improve your posture. There's nothing sexy about creeping about with hunched shoulders, head down and a nervous expression. Instead, stride out with shoulders back, chest forward, head up and chin down. Imagine a golden thread attached to the top of your head, which is lifting you up. Investigate having lessons in the Alexander Technique.

Make yourself sound more sexy. When we're nervous, we tend to gabble and speak quickly. So, if you want to sound irresistible, lower your voice and speak more slowly.

Wear clothes that will turn heads. Save that old polo neck and holey jeans for nights in with the girls. Or those joggers and baggy jumper for a night in with the boys. If you want to attract someone, you need clothes that will get you noticed. So invest in a stunning new dress or smart new suit for the next party you go to.

Girls, if you want to catch his eye, show just a tiny bit of flesh. Nothing too obvious. Just a glimpse of bare shoulder, or a cut-out back.

Look healthy. It's well documented that on a subconscious level, we're all drawn to partners whom we can imagine having babies with! That's why many men prefer women who are curvaceous. And women prefer fit, rugged, men who look as though they will protect them.

Tone up with a few sessions in the gym. The Teletubby look is not a turn-on. Don't let yourself go just because you're not dating. Join a health club, get fit and start a diet. That way, you'll be ready if you meet someone great. You'll also be more attractive.

Join the local residents' society. It's a good way to check out other singles in your area.

Go sailing. Being in close proximity to people for several days on a boat can make for some close encounters in the cabin.

Be brave and go on a singles vacation. Even if you don't meet the love of your life, you could make some great new friends.

Ask friends to set you up on a blind date.

Explore the whole new world of Internet dating. Thousands of singles are doing it now, so the chances of meeting that special someone are even greater. You may have to kiss a few frogs on the way, but persevere.

Walk the dog – it's a great ice-breaker and many a romance has sprung from Rover and Rosie getting friendly first! If you don't have a pooch, borrow one from a friend.

Love drama? – join a group. Seeing a play with others will immediately give you so much to talk about.

Help to save the environment and get involved in an eco-group. It's a wonderful way to meet other like-minded greenies.

Offer to help out an animal sanctuary at weekends to meet fellow animal-lovers.

Just because you haven't got anybody special in your life right now doesn't mean you're not open to the possibility of meeting someone new.

Smile. It makes you more approachable and few people can resist a smile.

When out on a date, mirror the other person's actions. This makes people subconsciously relax and open up, because they feel they're on the same wavelength as you.

If you're talking to someone new, keep conversations positive and uplifting. Listen to their verbal cues. Are they auditory (I feel what you mean), visual (I see what you mean), or kinaesthetic (touchy-feely types)? Try to communicate in the same way.

Now that you're on your own, make a list of what you value in a relationship. Establish what your standards are. For example, you expect a partner to be faithful and honest and you will not put up with abuse of any kind. These should be non-negotiables – no matter how good-looking she/he is, or how much she/he tells you he loves you.

If you want to meet a partner who is sporty, dynamic, adventurous or creative, start cultivating these qualities in yourself first. Often we're attracted to people because of qualities they have that we feel we don't have.

If you're finding it hard to move on emotionally after your break-up, a course of acupuncture, during which fine needles are inserted into acupoints along the body, can help rebalance your system. Traditional Chinese medicine recognizes that feelings of abandonment, rejection and being unloved can cause energy imbalances within the body. Acupuncture can help rectify this and promotes emotional recovery.

Try not to panic that you are on your own. Remind yourself of how well you coped before you met your partner.

If you've recently split up with a partner, it's natural to miss the elements that your other half brought into the relationship. For example, she was good with bills and social arrangements. Or he was handy at DIY and fixing the computer when it crashed. See if you can develop those skills in yourself now that you have a really good reason to. Becoming more self-reliant will further boost your self-esteem.

> *Friendship marks a life even more deeply than love. Love risks degenerating into obsession, friendship is never anything but sharing.*
>
> ELIE WIESEL

Trust your feelings when you meet someone new. They might seem perfectly charming and friendly. But if your sixth sense makes you feel uncomfortable – even if you can't explain this logically – go with your intuition.

Don't be shy and wait for others to make the first move. Always carry a few business cards with your e-mail address and phone number on, so the next time you meet someone you fancy, you can slip them your card.

Whenever you meet someone you've enjoyed talking to, drop them an e-mail or text within a couple of weeks or so. If you leave it too long to get in touch, the moment will pass. And you might miss out on making an interesting new friend.

Hang out at an Internet café. It's a good way to meet strangers.

A first date should be fun. So, keep schtum about your ex. You might think it makes a great story. But too much personal information, too soon, can be a major turn off. It smacks too much of – yawn – unresolved issues.

If you love someone, let them go. If they return to you, it was meant to be. If they don't, their love was never yours to begin with.

ANONYMOUS

Do what feels right for you. If the prospect of dating new people fills you with dread, it could be that you're simply not yet ready to move on. Just give yourself more time. It's better to hang back than launch into a new relationship on the rebound.

If you still feel bitter about a past relationship even though it ended some time ago, consider getting professional help. A course of counselling or psychotherapy could be exactly what you need to help you move on.

See an astrologer and have your birth chart analysed. This could help you understand your love life better. For example, it could tell you why you're attracted to certain types and explain the way you behave in relationships.

" *If you want to sacrifice the admiration of many men for the criticism of one, go ahead get married.* "
KATHARINE HEPBURN

Try this simple feng shui tactic for improving your love life. Put a pair of red candles in the south-west corner of your bedroom, which is linked to relationships. Red symbolizes blood and is considered a powerful magnet for love.

Improve your body image by taking up a fitness regime such as Pilates, Alexander Technique or yoga.

You never who you might meet when you're shuffling off to get the papers, looking less than glam, first thing on Sunday morning. So, make sure you always look clean, tidy and presentable – even if you're just popping out to the newsagent. Hair should be washed and shiny.

If you're at a party and feeling shy, try not to huddle in a corner with a friend. This may stop you meeting other people and making new friends. Make a pact that you will separate and try to talk to new people.

Relationships are like mirrors — like attracts like. For example, if you always seem to attract commitment-phobes, you may have a deep-seated fear of commitment within you. Or if you always seem to attract people who want to change you or put you down, could it be that you don't really accept yourself?

When you go on a date, leave your emotional baggage at home.

Be aware of body language. Notice if someone seems interested or whether their eyes are glazing over. And, if you want to attract someone, there are times when you have to make yourself slightly available. So don't cross your arms, or look the opposite way. This sends out totally the wrong signal and stops people from approaching you.

If you are a bit shy, try and relax and smile to make yourself seem more approachable, otherwise your aloofness may come over as rudeness.

> *A sense of duty is useful in work, but offensive in personal relations. People wish to be liked, not be endured with patient resignation.*
> BERTRAND RUSSELL

Look approachable. If you're with a group, don't cluster in a crowd as this is offputting. Instead, try and make it easier for potential admirers to join the group.

*Be flirtatious. Smile, look
people in the eye, tease a little
and show interest when
you're talking to someone.*

Don't pretend what you don't feel.
People will be able to sense it.

Don't try too hard.

Visualize your ideal partner. Focus on that image and believe that you can make your dream come true.

Don't just focus on finding a partner – enjoy making new friends of the opposite sex.

Go clubbing.

Go on a skiing holiday. It's a great way to meet some sporty good-lookers, especially when you're curled up in a chalet for a little après-ski.

Retain an air of mystery. It's human nature to be intrigued by the unknown and inscrutable. Think Greta Garbo.

*get the life
you want*

You don't know how long you'll be single for – so make the most of it while you can! This is your chance to grab every opportunity that comes your way and get the life you want. Being single means you've got so much more time to work out exactly what you want from life. That could be anything. If you've always wanted to change job, go travelling or set up your own business, now's the best time to do it. There's nothing and no one to stop you from pursuing your dreams. Do it now – before you fall in love again.

You've been given the opportunity, so now's your chance to reconnect with what you really feel passionate about. Start doing more of what it is you love. It could be anything: baking the most delicious cakes, getting excited about decorating your home, painting landscapes, buying and selling antiques or visiting new places.

Stop procrastinating. Try to work out why you keep putting things off. Often the worst procrastinators are secret perfectionists at heart. When you put things off, it's because you're terrified of not coming up to scratch. If this sounds like you, the sooner you stop trying to be perfect, the quicker you'll get things done.

You may be on your own – but don't put yourself down. This is counterproductive and will only stop you from achieving your goals.

Make a list of five things you want to achieve during the next year. Seeing things written down in black and white can act as a real incentive.

> *Happiness is not a matter of good fortune or worldly possessions. It's a mental attitude. It comes from appreciating what we have, instead of being miserable about what we don't have. It's so simple – yet so hard for the human mind to comprehend.*
>
> ANONYMOUS

Having come out of a relationship, it is a good time to reassess your plans for the future. Tell people your dreams and be open to any help and suggestions they offer.

If you've recently broken up with your partner, there will inevitably be moments when you feel sad and nostalgic. But if you can make a conscious effort to think more positively, this will help you to move on. If you've a tendency to self-doubt, this can seriously sabotage your efforts. Remember that like attracts like. Positive thinking attracts positive experiences. Not convinced? Try it for a couple of days and see what happens.

Look around you. There are bound to be people you know who have been through similar experiences and come through them stronger and happier. See what you can learn from them.

Getting ahead in a difficult profession requires avid faith in yourself. That is why some people with mediocre talent, but with great inner drive, go so much further than people with vastly superior talent.

SOPHIA LOREN

If you're looking to break with the past and change direction, find a mentor who will give you useful advice and support.

Always keep your goals in mind when you start a new project or activity.

Make a list of all the ways you would like to improve your life. Perhaps you want to work shorter hours, travel more, have more time for friends and family or write a book. Beside each point, write some suggestions of possible changes you could impose to make it happen. Seeing things written down on paper may be the spur you need.

" The secret of happiness is not in doing what one likes, but in liking what one does. "
JAMES M. BARRIE

Put the past behind you and redecorate your home. You don't have to spend a fortune: just give the place a fresh lick of paint. This is a good time to rethink your workspace, too. Working or living in a mess makes everything twice as difficult. It means you spend half your time trying to find things. So try and keep your workspace and home as streamlined as possible.

Even if it sometimes feels as if you're going it alone, don't give up too soon. A large part of being successful is due to perseverance.

> *When life's problems seem overwhelming, look around and see what other people are coping with. You may consider yourself fortunate.*
> ANN LANDERS

Focus on abundance – and stop thinking about what you haven't got. When you do this you will attract prosperity into your life.

Try to keep working weekends to a minimum and keep at least three evenings during the week work-free. If you're working more than that, what's the reason? Is it to block out the fact that there's no one to go home to? Perhaps you feel more vulnerable financially now that you're single again, and are more scared of losing your job. Whatever the reason, if you're spending more time working than living, you need to rethink your work commitments.

What would you wish for if you were granted three wishes? A loving relationship? A beautiful home? Think about what it is you most desire in life, as this can help you work out which areas you need to focus on.

If you feel low, or are just generally dissatisfied, try to bring more joy into your existence. If you take small steps to bring pleasure into your life, it doesn't matter if you can't step out of your situation immediately. The more positive you feel, the easier it will be to make changes.

66 *Opportunity ... often it comes in the form of misfortune, or temporary defeat.* 99
NAPOLEON HILL

With no one to delay you in the mornings, try getting into work 15 minutes earlier every day. This will give you time to plan the things you have to do that day and help you to feel more in control. It will also help you leave on time, so your evenings are free for fun.

When you're in a relationship, it's easy to forget about all the different things that you used to love doing when you were single. Now's your chance to rediscover them. Try incorporating new activities and interests into your life as much as you can.

Don't worry about only taking small steps to get to what you want. For example, even if you can only learn five new words in Spanish or Italian every day, think how many new words you'll know in a year. It all adds up eventually.

Always look on the bright side. There's nothing more draining than feeling anxious and worried. Thinking positively has an energizing effect. So instead of concentrating on everyday problems and hassles, try to look on the bright side. This may take practice at first, but you'll soon see how much easier life becomes when you do it.

> *Perfect happiness is not to look for happiness.*
> DEEPAK CHOPRA

Be daring. Instead of spending another weekend mooching around at home, book a weekend in Marrakech, learn to ski or scuba-dive. You won't regret trying something new. You'll only regret the things you haven't done.

Plan to make your working life more personally satisfying. This might not happen overnight, but if you are open to change, you're more likely to attract new opportunities.

Think of a place you've always dreamed of visiting, then work out how you can get there. Perhaps you need to save up for it first. Maybe you have something you could sell to fund your trip. If you put your mind to it, you can be there sooner than you think.

We've all heard people described as larks or owls. These terms came about as a result of animal studies which showed that being a morning or evening person has a lot to do with genetic inheritance. So, work out your own best personal rhythms and plan accordingly. You may be at your most creative late at night. If you know you're at your sparkiest in the morning, and you want to go running at 6a.m., who's to stop you?

Do all the tasks you least enjoy first. That way, your day gets easier as you go along.

When you're single, you won't get very far by holding back. So don't just stay on the sidelines and wait for things to happen. If you want to live life to the full, you need to get involved.

> *Remember that overnight success usually takes about 15 years.*
> ANONYMOUS

If you stop comparing yourself to others, this will free you up to do what you really want.

Follow your own path,
not the one your parents,
friends or ex-partner
envisaged for you.

*Don't just bumble through life
– try and spend a few minutes
every day focusing on what it is
you want to achieve.*

" *All of us have the capacity to attract to ourselves
what seems to be missing in our lives.* "
DR WAYNE DYER

Reorganize your clothes. Separate everything into sections such as skirts, dresses, jackets, trousers, shirts, T-shirts, tops, shoes, boots and bags. You'll have fun finding things you'd forgotten you had. If you find things that no longer fit, pass them on to a friend who admired them, or use them as motivation for a new fitness and diet plan.

" Aim at heaven and you will get earth thrown in.
Aim at earth and you get neither. "
C. S. LEWIS

Stop trying to be perfect and accept yourself for who you are.

66 *Choose a job you love, and you will never have to work a day in your life.* 99
CONFUCIUS

Keep going. Don't ditch a dream just because you come up against a few obstacles. If you can work through these, you'll be glad you did when you start to reap the rewards.

Believe that things will work out for you.

Be patient – and that includes in your love life. It's better to wait a while for what you want than to give up and miss out in the long run.

Don't be scared to ask others for advice.

Do your research. For example, if you want to retrain for a new career, take a college course or go horse-trekking in the Andes, make sure you have all the information you need.

With no one to rely on but yourself, you'll feel more secure if you can get your finances under control. Make a start by sorting out your debts. Not owing money is very liberating. See if you can start saving a little each month. And investigate your pension – the earlier you start saving, the bigger it will be.

If you're finding it difficult to get started on a project, focus on making one small step to begin with. This is less scary than thinking of the whole picture and will help you to get you going. Don't take on more than you can deliver. It's better to do a few things well than lots of things badly.

Keep a diary to track your progress. Log your activities day by day. Seeing a full diary is a great motivator.

Don't take on so much that you feel stressed all the time.

Make a list of short-term and long-term goals.

Just because you haven't got a partner, that doesn't mean you can't have a dream holiday. Go with a friend and see how much fun it can be.

Try and maintain a good work-life balance. Don't let work take over your life. If you need help, ask for it; always take regular breaks. Make sure you leave yourself enough time to relax and spend time on other activities or just hanging out with friends.

With only yourself to answer to, don't be scared to change your mind about something.

A journey of 1,000 miles begins with a single step.

LAO TZU

Let desire become intention. In other words, don't just dream it, do it.

Dare to be different.

Be curious about life; explore and ask questions.

Even if you feel you're going through a rough time, recognize that you can always improve your life.

Don't let anyone discourage you or throw you off course, but on the other hand, listen to wise advice.

GET THE LIFE YOU WANT   255

An Hachette Livre Company
First published in Great Britain in 2008 by MQ Publications,
a division of Octopus Publishing Company Ltd
2–4 Heron Quays, London E14 4JP

www.octopusbooks.co.uk

ISBN: 978-1-84601-242-6

10 9 8 7 6 5 4 3 2 1

Printed and bound in China

This book contains the opinions and ideas of the author. It is intended to
provide helpful and informative material on the subjects addressed in this
book and is sold with the understanding that the author and publisher are
not engaged in rendering medical, health, or any other kind of personal
professional services in this book. The reader should consult his or her
medical, health, or competent professional before adopting any of the
suggestions in this book or drawing references from it. The author and
publisher disclaim all responsibility for any liability, loss, or risk, personal
or otherwise, which is incurred as a consequence, directly or indirectly, of
the use and application of any of the contents of this book.